Portage Public Library

DEC 7 - 1992

10.41

S0-FQM-085

Responsible Pet Care

Ducks

Responsible Pet Care

Ducks

CARLIENNE FRISCH

Rourke Publications, Inc.
Vero Beach, FL 32964

© **1991 Rourke Publications, Inc.**

All rights reserved. No part of this book may be reproduced or utilized in any form or by any means, electronic or mechanical including photocopying, recording or by any information storage and retrieval system without permission in writing from the publisher.

Library of Congress Cataloging-in-Publication Data

Frisch, Carlienne, 1944–
    Ducks / by Carlienne A. Frisch
      p. cm.–(Responsible pet care)
    Includes bibliographical references (p.).
    Summary: Discusses the selection of a duck as a pet and how to house, feed, handle, groom, and breed it.
    ISBN 0-86625-192-8
    1. Ducks as pets–Juvenile literature.   [1. Ducks as pets.]
I. Title. II. Series: Responsible pet care (Vero Beach, Fla.)
SF505.3.F75 1991
636.5'97–dc20   90-9092
                                                                        CIP
                                                                         AC

CONTENTS

1	Why Choose A Duck?	6
2	Varieties of Ducks	8
3	Choosing Your Ducks	10
4	Shelter and Housing	12
5	Equipment	14
6	Feeding	16
7	Grooming and Handling	18
8	Ailments	20
9	Breeding	22
10	Incubation	24
11	Ducklings	26
12	Exhibiting Your Ducks	28
	Glossary	30
	Index	31

Is A Duck For You?

A duck is not likely to be a cuddly pet. Because it normally lives in a flock, or group, of ducks when in the wild, it prefers the company of other ducks. It may let the family cat or dog make friends with it, but only if the duck keeps the "upper hand." It is unlikely to become as attached to its owner as a cat or dog would.

A duck will eat a varied diet of plants, insects, grains, and commercial poultry **feed**. It can live in a protected area of your yard or on a nearby pond. Ducks can live without a swimming area, but are happier if given a place to swim.

In the past, fancy breeds were kept mainly by royalty. As the number of wild ducks increased over the years, farmers **domesticated** ducks, or began breeding them for food. Today, about 15 million ducks are raised each year in the United States, mostly for food. Ducks may live up to 20 years, although most live only two to five years.

Wild mallards are the ancestors of all domestic North American ducks, except the Muscovy.

A duck's feet are shaped like paddles. This helps the duck swim—and gives it a distinctive waddle on land.

The term duck includes both males, called drakes, and females, called hens. Drakes usually have the most colorful feathers.

Ducks are waterfowl. They are members of the family Anatidae, which also includes geese and swans. Ducks' bodies are designed for life on the water. Under their skin is a layer of fat to give them warmth and buoyancy in the water. A layer of very soft feathers, called **down**, lies under their outer feathers and helps keep ducks warm and dry. Their outer feathers are covered with a natural oil that makes them waterproof.

A duck's short, thin legs and paddle-shaped feet with three webbed toes make it a strong, natural swimmer, but it waddles clumsily on land. A wild duck has powerful wings that give it speed and grace in the air.

The average duck measures 17 to 21 inches from the tip of its bill to the end of its tail, and weighs one-and-one-half to three pounds. Domestic ducks are usually larger and more comfortable around people than wild ducks. Both types, however, can make interesting pets.

Varieties of Ducks

There are about 50 species, or kinds, of ducks. Of those species, 22 are sea ducks, which live on the cold northern coasts of oceans. There are 14 species of fresh water ducks that live on ponds, marshes, rivers, and lakes, and in the grasses near them. The 13 species of perching ducks make their nests in holes in trees.

Sea ducks are large and usually brightly colored. They include the merganser, goldeneye, and eider. They eat shellfish, sea urchins, squid, and fish. However, they are not usually kept as pets in the United States.

Fresh water ducks are medium-sized. They include the mallard, the canvasback, and the ringneck. These ducks are the most common.

Wood ducks are perching ducks, which means they make their nests in trees. The male (left) has much brighter markings than the female (right). A Canadian goose is in the background.

The American widgeon is a dabbler. It dips its head into shallow water in order to reach food.

Perching ducks, such as the wood duck, the mandarin, and the Muscovy, usually have colorful feathers. The nests of some perching ducks are as much as 60 feet from the ground.

Ducks also are separated into two groups according to how they catch their food. Some ducks, such as the mallard and teal, are called **dabblers**. They stretch their necks to feed on the bottom of a shallow pond or marsh. The two parts of the bill are called the **mandibles**. The edges of each mandible in a dabbler's bill have sharp "teeth" similar to the cutting edge of a saw. Their tongue is thick and also has edges like a saw. The edges on the bill and tongue help the duck get and eat food. Dabblers take off from the water by jumping and pushing down with their wings.

Other ducks, such as the canvasback and ringneck, are called diving ducks. These ducks have long, narrow, pointed bills. They dive to the bottom of a deeper lake or river for their food. Divers swim under water with their wings closed and their legs sticking out to their sides. They must run along the surface of the water to take off flying because their wings are small for the size of their bodies.

Choosing Your Ducks

You may get ducks from a farmer, another pet owner, or a hatchery. If you get ducklings, or baby ducks, you must give them more care than adult ducks. The number of ducks you get will depend on housing space, water area, feed costs, cost of the ducks, and how much time you want to spend with your birds.

Look for healthy ducks that are active and have clear eyes. Their heads will not droop. Their droppings should not be too watery or have blood in them.

Most ducks don't like to be held and don't follow people except at feeding time. Muscovy, mandarin, and call hens, however, may become true pets. They easily adapt to people.

Although most domesticated breeds are too heavy to fly, domestic mallards, calls, and young Muscovys can fly very well. To keep them from leaving, the owner must confine them or must trim, or "clip," their wings.

Although Muscovys are raised mainly for their meat, they adapt well to people and can make good pets. This is a Muscovy male, or drake.

After living near people for several generations, mallards lose their instinct to migrate.

Although the Muscovy is raised mainly for its meat, the hen will lay about 50 eggs a year. Muscovys perch on barns, houses, fences, and trees. In a building, the hen will choose a shelf on the wall for a nest location. Interestingly, this breed hisses rather than quacks.

The mandarin, also a perching duck, is one of the most beautiful of the fancy breeds. Its chestnut, blue-green, and copper-green coloring may fade, however, in domesticated birds. Though small, the mandarin is ready to defend itself against much larger breeds.

The call, a bantam breed, is the smallest domesticated duck, weighing only 18 ounces. In the past, its loud voice made it useful as a hunting decoy. Today, it makes an unusual pet.

If you have a pond and don't care to tame your ducks, mallards are a good choice. They live on and near fresh water, eating plants, insects, and small water animals. After a few generations of living near people, mallards lose their **instinct** to **migrate**, or fly to another area seasonally. If wild mallards are nearby, however, the domesticated birds may leave with them.

11

Shelter And Housing

Ducks are not as hardy as geese and swans in cold climates. Where temperatures go below freezing, ducks need to have shelter during the winter. This protects them from frostbite on their feet and from hungry **predators**.

During the winter, you may confine a duck in any predator-proof building. Be sure there is good ventilation, a constant water supply, feed, and artificial lighting. A dirt floor is best. Give each duck at least four square feet of space. You should also place individual wooden nesting boxes along the floor or on the wall, depending on your breed of duck. Make each box 14 inches wide, 18 inches long, and 14 inches high. The duck will make a nest from a supply of dry hay and its own feathers.

All sorts of birds share this winter shelter and penned area—including ducks, geese, chickens, and wild turkeys.

Ducks like to get into closed-in areas. Propped together, these hay bales make a good nesting place for a duck.

Make sure the water container is large enough to hold plenty of water. Use a water heater to keep the water from freezing. When ducks are not on open swimming water, they depend on their owner for drinking water.

Place the water supply on a screened stand over a floor drain or container that will collect spilled water. This keeps the floor from becoming too wet and creating a humid environment.

During warmer weather, ducks will thrive in a penned area, called a run. Its top and sides should be sturdy wire mesh to keep out predators, especially at night. A small portable pen will house two or three ducks and can be moved every few days to a clean grassy area. If predators are a problem, two or three ducks may be shut up for the night in a small dog house with a secure door to keep them safe until morning. Make sure they have a supply of water and feed. It's important to provide a shaded area for your ducks during warm weather.

Equipment

Ducks don't require much equipment. All they really need is a feeder and a waterer. You may also want a cage to take your birds to poultry exhibitions. A small cage works well for moving a young duck. Use a large cage when moving several ducks or to keep two ducks together for breeding. A cage set up on blocks outdoors also makes a house that lets droppings fall to the ground.

A cage for traveling should be large enough so the ducks aren't crowded. The top should be low enough, however, to keep the ducks from standing. If they stand, they may lose their balance and injure themselves.

Plastic or metal troughs are the most common feeders for young ducks. As the birds grow, you can use a self-feeder such as a hanging tube feeder. If possible, put it outdoors to keep spilled feed out of the shelter. A feed store manager can advise you on the proper feeder size, which depends on how many ducks you have and how often you are able to fill the feeder.

Duck equipment doesn't have to be fancy or expensive. A simple homemade feeder can work just fine.

Ducks are happiest when they can swim. A pond or lake is best, but you can make a small swimming area out of a wading pool or tank.

Young ducks need a waterer that is deep enough to put their bills in up to the nostril. The waterer must not be wide enough for them to get into, however, or they'll make a mess. Ducklings should not be given open water pans until they are completely feathered. If their down gets soaked, they may die. For older ducks, it's best to use water pans covered by a grill that lets them drink, but won't let them get in and make the water dirty. In cold climates, drinking water should be kept from freezing by using a rod heater. The cords should be placed where the ducks won't trip over them and unplug the heater.

Ducks that swim will be healthier, lay more and better eggs, have cleaner feathers, and need less feed. You can make a swimming area out of a large, low tank or even a child's wading pool. A natural pond, of course, is the best kind of swimming area.

15

Feeding

Mallards on a pond will eat a variety of wild plants, berries, and grains, as well as insects, tadpoles, worms, snails, and small fish. During winter months, put a feeder near the water's edge. You can use an oversized birdfeeder with an overhanging top to keep out snow or rain. Hang the feeder on a post driven into the bottom of the pond. Keep the feeder supplied with pellets or grain. If the pond freezes over completely, you'll have to provide your ducks with water.

If your ducks run loose in your yard, they may come to the door at mealtime, demanding food. They'll let you know when they are hungry! In addition to their diet of plants, insects, worms, and snails, adult ducks benefit from eating poultry feed pellets. Grains also are good, but take longer to digest. If you do not want to buy pellets, mix a feed of equal parts cracked corn, wheat, and oats. It's better not to feed mash, or ground grain, because it is not easy for ducks to swallow and much is wasted. It is important to always have water available near the feed.

These hungry mallards are looking for tadpoles or small fish. Ducks eat a variety of other foods as well, including plants and insects.

Poultry feed pellets provide ducks with essential nutrients. The duck in the foreground is a mandarin; the others are Rouens, also called brown mallards.

If you have ducklings, feed should be ready for them as soon as they arrive or are hatched. If they are with the mother duck, she will teach them to **forage** for insects and other protein, and to feed from dishes. If they are indoors and cannot forage, feed them a 22-percent protein starter ration of the poultry feed. You may be able to buy duckling starter rations, but you can use chick starter that is not medicated. It's important to know that some medications in chick feed are toxic to ducks and may poison your ducklings.

Ducklings will eat mash easily, but they may choke on pellets or grains until they reach three weeks of age. Some types of ducklings, such as calls, are so small that they cannot have pellets for eight weeks. It is best to give them moistened mash at first and to add grass at two weeks. Because call ducklings are so small, they cannot be raised with ducklings of other species. They will be pushed away from the feed, and may also be trampled by the larger birds.

Grooming And Handling

A duck grooms, or **preens**, itself very well. It arranges its feathers by shaking its body from tail to head and then smoothing the ruffled feathers with its bill. The bill repeatedly passes over a gland near the tail that produces oil. The oil, spread on the feathers, keeps them waterproof. While preening, the duck also removes insects with its bill. Keep an eye out for any duck that quits preening. A sick or injured duck may not preen itself. As the oil wears off, water will seep through to the skin and the duck will get cold. If it is cold for too long, it will die.

At the end of summer, ducks shake their wings and the feathers drop out. This is called **molting**. Ducks cannot fly until new feathers grow in. Mallards molt in early summer as well as in late summer. All summer, the mallard drake's feathers are brown like the hen's. He grows colorful feathers again in the autumn.

This buff domestic mallard has started to molt its wing feathers. New feathers will soon replace the old ones.

When holding a duck, make sure its wings are kept close to its body.

Because most ducks are not used to handling, it is not easy to catch one to clip its wings, move it to another location, or attend to its health. It is best to plan ahead. Ducks that are fed regularly can be taught to go into a pen or building for their feed, where they will be easier to catch.

To pick up a duck, stand behind the bird. With your right hand, take hold of the right wing where it meets the duck's body. At the same time, gently push the duck to the ground. Immediately bring the duck up to your body with the left wing against your chest. Slide your right hand out from under the wing and put it over the wing. Put your left arm around the top of the breast and your left hand over the right wing.

Muscovy drakes are so large and strong that they can seriously injure a careless handler with their wings. To pick up a Muscovy drake, come up from behind and take hold of the right wing near the body with your right hand. With the left hand, take hold of the left wing near the drake's body. Lift the bird and hold his back firmly to your chest.

Ailments

Ducks are easy to raise because they do not get many poultry diseases. There are, however, some problems for which the duck owner should contact a veterinarian or the state poultry laboratory.

Enteritis, or duck plague, is a contagious disease caused by a herpes virus. Symptoms include thirst, watery or bloody diarrhea, listlessness, poor appetite, droopy wings, and swollen eyelids. Although there is no treatment for this usually fatal disease, it can be prevented by keeping pens clean. It's also important to immediately remove any sick-looking ducks.

These mallards have made their home in a park.

A mallard stretches its wings after a good rest.

Botulism, also called limberneck and western duck sickness, is a fatal, non-contagious food poisoning that ducks get when they eat decaying plants, spoiled grains, or infected maggots. If you discover it before the neck, legs, and wings become paralyzed, flush out the duck with a solution of epsom salts followed by potassium permanganate. The duck must also be taken to a veterinarian to get antitoxin injections to prevent further paralysis and death. The source of the poison should be searched for and removed.

Cholera affects ducks over six weeks of age. They will have yellow-green diarrhea, fever, depression, ruffled feathers, watery eyes, and fast breathing. A rattle in the throat and swollen joints will soon follow. You can treat cholera with sulfa drugs or prevent it by vaccination.

No one should ever eat the meat of a duck that died from a disease or had to be killed because it was sick.

Breeding

If you want to hatch ducklings, you will need a drake to make a hen's eggs fertile. If he is not of the same species as the hen, the ducklings will be sterile **hybrids**. They will not be able to produce ducklings of their own.

Select your breeding ducks about a month before you want to start egg production. A hen should be at least seven months old, and the drake should be a bit older. You can put up to six hens with the drake. Feed a breeder-layer ration. Feeding ground oystershell is not necessary, but may make the shells stronger.

Most ducks lay eggs in the early morning. Ducks are not particular where they drop their eggs, so it is best to shut them in a clean, dry, well-ventilated building until they have laid that day's egg. They need nest boxes of at least 14 x 18 x 14 inches and nesting material. Sod or dirt makes a good nest bottom. These materials keep the eggs cool and prevent them from drying too fast. Straw may let the eggs slide out, and hay may begin to rot during **incubation** and spoil the eggs. Give each duck five or six feet of floor space and a constant supply of food and water. Clean **litter** on the floor will help the duck produce clean eggs.

These ducks are wild mallards. The drake is on the left, and the hen on the right. For breeding, a hen should be at least 7 months old, and the drake a little older.

The four ducks pictured here are different colors and sizes, but they are all domestic mallards. From left to right: a buff, or khaki, mallard; a snowy mallard; a white mallard; and a Rouen, sometimes called a brown mallard.

When the ducks have gone out for the day, collect the eggs and wash soiled ones in water that is at least 20 degrees F. warmer than the eggs. Add a commercial egg-cleaning solution. Keep the eggs at 50–55 degrees and at a relative humidity of 75 percent, perhaps in your basement. Do not stack them up or place them inside an egg carton, and don't save cracked eggs. Place them in a single layer in an open box or tray. If you store eggs for more than a week, turn them once a day to prevent the yolks from sticking to the inside of the shells. When you have about 10 eggs per hen, return them to the nests for the hens to set on and hatch. If a hen is reluctant to leave a nest when you are gathering eggs, especially toward the end, put about 10 eggs into her nest and let her begin setting. She will not know if you have given her the eggs she laid or those of another hen.

23

Incubation

When a hen hatches ducklings herself, that is natural incubation or **brooding**. The owner's only responsibility is to provide food, water, and protection from predators. The duck will set on the eggs for about a month after her last egg was laid. Muscovy eggs hatch after 35 days; the eggs of other domestic duck breeds take 28 days.

Ducks may abandon their nests if frightened or after only a few ducklings have hatched. The remaining eggs can be hatched in an incubator if they have not gotten too cold. However, you should candle each egg to make sure each duckling is alive. To do this, cut a small hole—a bit smaller than an egg—in the bottom of a shoe box. Place the box upside-down over a small, bright light in a darkened room. Set an egg in the hole so that the light shines up through the egg. You should be able to see movement in the egg and the air sac at the egg's wide end. If you put the egg to your ear, you may hear peeping. If you do not at least see the outline of a duckling, discard the egg, as it is not fertile.

After setting begins, it takes about 28 days for a duck's eggs to hatch.

It's all right to use hay or straw in nesting boxes if you collect the eggs every day.

Preheat a commercial incubator for the eggs. Put a warm, wet towel in the bottom of the tray under the eggs for moisture. Stand the eggs on end with the air cell upward. You can prop the eggs with stones. Mist the eggs lightly with water and close the lid. At first, check the temperature every few minutes. The temperature at the top of the incubator should be 101–102 degrees F. In an incubator with a fan that circulates the air, 95–98 degrees is ideal.

To keep from opening the incubator, check the temperature with an oral thermometer through a vent hole in the incubator. A pen hygrometer can be used to check the humidity level. Look for a 90–92 degrees F. wet-bulb reading.

Hatching will usually begin in six hours and be completed the next day. Eggs that cooled off somewhat before being placed in the incubator will take longer to hatch.

Ducklings

A duckling hammers its way out of the shell and enters the world with blinking eyes and wet feathers. In an hour, it becomes dry, soft, and downy.

The hen will oil her ducklings' down before leading them into any water. If they wander away from their mother in the yard, they may drown in water from which they cannot get out. Therefore, it is important to keep all water containers more than one-inch deep out of reach of the ducklings. The hen may not get them out of the water because she did not lead them into it.

A mother duck usually accepts extra ducklings from the incubator or from another hen that has died. Truly orphaned ducklings can be raised under a heat lamp. A veterinarian or farm supply store manager can tell you if this is necessary.

A duckling sleeps with its bill tucked under its wing.

A young American widgeon takes a long drink from a pond. In a few months the colors on its head will be much brighter.

The hen teaches the ducklings how to forage for food and how to avoid most predators. Even the strong Muscovy drake, which stays with the hen (unlike drakes of other breeds), cannot turn away all predators. The owner must provide a secure shelter, especially at night.

At about three weeks, ducklings begin to grow brownish-gray feathers. After 10 weeks, they can fly and are called **fledglings**.

Ducklings may get hepatitis, or baby duck disease. A vaccine will prevent this highly contagious disease. The sick duckling will lie on its side with its head under its tail and its feet paddling. Hepatitis is fatal in birds under four weeks of age.

New duck disease affects ducklings up to eight weeks of age. They cough and sneeze, have green diarrhea, have a shaky head and neck, and lose their balance. This contagious disease usually is fatal in ducklings, unless treated early with antibiotics.

Exhibiting Your Ducks

If you plan to exhibit your ducks at fairs or poultry shows, you will want several birds from which to choose. Make your final choices one month before the show. During that time, confine the show ducks. Give them clean litter, clean drinking water, and a bathing pen so they can keep themselves clean. Get them used to activity and handling by spending a lot of time with them.

Birds with colored feathers must be kept out of the sun so their feathers won't fade. If the birds happen to molt before the show, however, the judge will take that into consideration.

The day before the show, remove the bathing pen. Pluck faded or off-color feathers—do not cut feathers or trim the **crest**. Using a soft-bristled fingernail brush dipped into water and a small amount of hydrogen peroxide, gently scrub dirt from the ducks' legs, feet, and claws. Carefully remove dirt from the sensitive bill and nostrils using plain water and a soft cloth. You can gently remove stubborn dirt from nostrils with a toothpick.

Muscovys come in many color combinations, and are often exhibited at county fairs.

The bill of this Rouen would have to be cleaned before it's brought to a show.

Clean any dirty feathers with a small amount of shampoo and water. Rinse by wiping with a wet cloth. Never rub feathers except in the direction they grow. Apply a bit of vegetable, mineral, or cod-liver oil on the ducks' legs. You can shine their bills and claws with a nail buffer.

The cage for transporting, and the cage you plan to use at the show, should both be large enough so the birds will not touch the sides. Feathers that touch the cage sides may break off.

At the show, attach a couple of medium-size coffee cans into corners of the show cage with wire. You can put pellets in one and water in the other. This arrangement will help keep the cage—and your duck—dry and clean.

Showing your ducks, and maybe winning a ribbon, is a great reward for all your efforts!

GLOSSARY

Brood, brooding — To set upon eggs to be hatched. A brood is also a group of birds hatched at one time.

Crest — A natural growth on top of a bird's head.

Dabblers — Ducks that catch their food by dipping their heads in and out of the water.

Domesticated — To be made tame through careful breeding.

Down — Soft, fine feathers.

Fledglings — Young ducks that fly for the first time.

Forage — To search for, and eat, natural food.

Hybrids — The offspring of two birds of different species. The hybrid is usually not able to produce offspring.

Incubation — Keeping eggs warm so they will hatch.

Instinct — A natural tendency that a bird or animal has, inborn in the species.

Litter — Material used for bedding.

Mandible — Each part of the duck's bill.

Migrate — To move from one region to another with a change of seasons.

Molting — Dropping old feathers at certain times of the year and replacing them with new feathers.

Predators — Animals or birds that hunt and kill other animals or birds for food.

Preen — To clean and smooth feathers with the bill.

INDEX

Ailments	20, 21, 27	Illness	18, 20, 21
		Incubation	22, 24
Bathing	28	Incubator	24, 25
Bills	9, 28		
Breeding	22	Life span	6
Breeds	8		
		Molting	18
Cage	14, 29		
Cleaning	20, 28, 29	Nesting boxes	12, 22
Color	11	Nests	9, 11, 12, 22
Diet	6, 8, 16	Pens	13
Drakes	7, 22	Perching ducks	11
Ducklings	26	Pond	6, 11, 15
		Preening	18
Eggs	22, 23, 24, 25		
Equipment	12, 13, 14, 15	Shelter	12
Exhibiting	28, 29	State poultry laboratory	20
		Swimming	6, 15
Feathers	7, 18, 28, 29		
Feeders	14, 16	Traveling	14
Feet	7, 28		
Flock	6	Varieties of ducks	8
Food	16, 17, 22	Veterinarian	20, 21, 26
Grooming	18	Water	6, 13, 15, 16, 26
		Wings	7, 10
Handling	10, 19		
Health	10		
Hens	7, 26, 27		

31

Photographs by Mark E. Ahlstrom

*We would like to thank the following people
for their help in making this book:*

Shawn Lang
Alan Tilson

Produced by Mark E. Ahlstrom
(The Bookworks)
St. Peter, MN

Typesetting and Keylining: The Final Word
Photo Research: Judith A. Ahlstrom

Ducks /
J 636.597 F

318148500B9712

Frisch, Carlienne,
PORTAGE PUBLIC LIB   10544

J636.597   DEC 7 - 1992   Por.
  F
        Frisch, Carlienne
            Ducks

Portage Public Library